Rain Witness

Rain Witness

Poems by

Ed Ryterband Ph.D.

© 2022 Ed Ryterband. All rights reserved.
This material may not be reproduced in any form, published,
reprinted, recorded, performed, broadcast,
rewritten or redistributed without
the explicit permission of Ed Ryterband.
All such actions are strictly prohibited by law.

Cover design, original art by Michael Ryterband

ISBN: 978-1-63980-208-1

Kelsay Books
502 South 1040 East, A-119
American Fork, Utah 84003
Kelsaybooks.com

*Dedicated to my friends and colleagues
at US1/DV Poets Cooperative
who have provided consistent encouragement
and candid feedback
that has made these poems
truer to their original intent
and better music.*

Acknowledgments

Thanks to those who have helped me find nourishment in noticing and unpacking scraps of my experience so they might become these poems. As I said in the Dedication, my fellow poets in US1/DV Poets Cooperative have been a steady source of useful critique of the poems included here.

My wife, Madelyne, is again my favorite muse (and critic). She reminds me to not get attached to the outcome of writing, just engage freely and persevere. I have done so. Each of the poems has come out of a long engagement where I discovered, with her help, more about what they wanted to say.

Looking back, I have a debt to Nancy Scott, who I've worked with for many years and who has admonished me to not *over-write*. Nancy was for many years the Editor of *US1 Worksheets* and in 2021 published *A Little Excitement,* poems to blunt the ravages of the pandemic.

This past year saw the passing of Nancy, as well as Sondra Gash, my coach for ten years and author of her inspiring volume *Silk Elegy*. I am deeply grateful for her warm, insightful encouragement. Finally, Stephen Dunn has also left us. He was a teacher in my reading (and rereading) his poems, in his writing about poetry (*Walking Light*), and in his personal coaching.

Most of the poems here are new; some are updates of previous work. These updates are here because they've been extensively revised to become better messengers of what those poems wanted to say.

Contents

Prologue

Rain Witness   15

I. Connections

Night Cruller	19
The Looks of Love	21
Time and You	22
Sequester Memory	23
Sunday in the Pandemic with Michael	24
Their Suitcase in the Attic	26
Affair Overture	28
Anniversary	30
Loved One	32
Mother's Still	33

II. Religion and Politics

Being First	37
The Hand of God	38
Dust Bowl Troubadour	40
Grandmother of God	41
Having It Out with My Guru about Old Age	43
I Come from a Long Line Of	45
That Morning in the Queen of Peace Church	46
Narcissus' Deal with the Foxes and the Weasels	48
The Times Square Prophet	50
Work Autumn Epiphany	52

III. Meditations

Autumn Moment	57
Deep Night Elegy	59
Giraffe Whisperer	61
Late Winter Blues	63
Mid-Day Musings	64
Ode to Stargazer Lilies	66
Retreat with *The New Yorker*	67
Miracle of the Cantaloupes	68
The Wisdom of Tuning into Bill Evans	70

IV. Aging

Big Boys Come Home	73
Empty Nest Arrangements	74
I Think about the Lobster	75
Meeting Up with Never	77
Old Timer	78
Our Dying	80
Resolutions	82
Fort Lauderdale Dilemma	83
What I Will Be	85
An Ode to My Older Brother	87

V. Epilogue

How I Keep Me Going	91

Prologue

Rain Witness

I am safe and still
inside the discreet beauty of this moment
wrap myself in the early autumn rain
resign the past
pay nothing to the future

choose to be just here
witness on our back porch
the forest fifty feet away
a billion rain drops
announce themselves upon a million leaves.

I flow
into see-through sheets of rain
cascade with them
down the trees

greet sporadic chirps and squawks
from unseen birds
then turn back
into the rainfall.

The scene unfolds
one minute
then the next.

I sit here
on our back porch
still a witness

look out
listen

disappear.

I.
Connections

Night Cruller

In their bedroom he and she
lay down
in their chosen sides
drop off into their separate sleep

begin their wheezes
cover tussles
snorts begetting mid-sleep interruptions
when he'd lurch out for the bathroom

in the trance learned long ago
ending when
he'd slip politely
back into his half

except this night
he lifts the cover
slow and careful
creeps across the great divide

feels her
bites her shoulder
soothes it with his lips
wiggles close until

voila, she wiggles back.
Without a word
they twist their bodies into one
this giant cruller . . .

He whispers close into her ear
You are my food
my just dessert.
He smiles to himself
she must be smiling too.

The Looks of Love

In the beginning our raw erotic clamor
phosphoric flashes
overcame our doubts
bestowed us hungry nights and mornings
craving wonders
in each other's flesh.

Then came fateful choices
donations of our blood and futures into babies
aliens who conquered spaces we once called our own.
We reveled in their laughter, their triumphs.
The years helped us to forget
their cries, demands and disappointments.

Now our mirror shows this older couple
who've kept on all these years
worn smooth like stones in rivers
rounded from the flow of countless days.
We touch each other still
less frequent, more distracted.

We've journeyed all these places
sometimes self-immersed and restless.
We worry to each other, to ourselves
keep on showing up because
we said we would
choose to still believe
there will be ways to love ahead.

Time and You

I want you
my tenured partner
to show you love me still
embolden me

be advocate and audience
maybe critic
when I share my reruns
my burnished conquests and rebellions.

Time's wicked finger pokes me
and you are here each morning
help me stare it down
or stay distracted.

Your voice, your look, laughter, tears
channel me to moments
I search for to forget
I'm in a life that ends

without you
a time I give infrequent notice
until it surely will arrive
foist itself upon me
like a cat upon an unsuspecting mouse.

Sequester Memory

You come back
from deep inside
that album *The Early Years.*

I hold the old print photo
you pose in homemade costumes
a spaceman and big bird

artless smiles for the camera
before we take you by the hand
down the street to trick or treat.

You've been
down within the basement
in that old maple bookcase

my pile up of keepsakes
ignored until this time of virus
when remembering is not an anodyne routine.

Today I searched for you
looked back again
found the four of us
inside our once upon a time.

Sunday in the Pandemic with Michael

We'd surrendered
the freedom to be careless
had not hugged, or held

or smelled our sons in months
until our Brooklyn boy
resolves to risk New Jersey

dares an hour's drive to us
navigates a million unseen hazards
with his sweetheart.

On the back porch
Mom and Dad are here, Mike and Drea there.
Snacks and chatter try to span the social distance.

Suddenly he shuts his eyes
cloaks his face inside his hands
his shoulders shake.

She reaches for him
her hand rests lightly on his arm.
She looks up, over to us.

He wanted you to know
he misses hugging you
And we are engaged.

Mikey's going to be married.
Now everyone is joy struck, sobbing
despite the freedom lost.

No touching
even later
as they say good bye.

Their Suitcase in the Attic

In a corner of the attic
Mom and Dad's gray suitcase
the stiff old kind, no wheels
from another time
when the people in my family were alive.

Their initials, M and J, on crusted latches
I pull to open up the lid,
set free mold smells from the fabric pockets
unpack old photos, them and us two boys
wrapped in yellowed newsprint.

Mom smiles, shy, polite
her hands, arthritis still in hiding
rest on that blue dress, smooth and shiny
covered in pink roses I once tried to smell.
Gone 2004.

Dad glows triumphant in his open collar shirt
one hand on his rod and reel, taller than he is
the other holds his trophy dolphin
before the War and I arrived.
Gone 2006.

Brother Mel looks right into the camera
red-haired cherub freckles cover fat and rosy cheeks.
A Gerber Baby twin
once slept in a bed nearby mine.
Gone 2020.

The growing sting inside my eyes
the dry swallow
tell me I should linger
inside memories I can remake
as fond as my desires.

I see them
feel them
chat in whispers with them
until I wrap them up
tuck them neatly back into the suitcase.

Affair Overture

He's on alert
scans across that crowded room
makes furtive note
her shoulder turns
her smile, a nod
could be in his direction.

Maybe is sufficient.

He slows his breath
contemplates his age, mature
his circumstance, substantial
his wit, his skill in grooming
planting kindnesses
sugar fabrications.

He hugs the tension.

Calculates what next
to say, to do
wonders
if he might attract, repel
cause only mild interest
his hope-filled moment quickly vaporized.

He closes the debate.

Ventures outward to his invitation
a rendevous at lunch
a public place
where he can bob and weave
inspect her answers
to his unannounced desires.

He hopes to free his craving.

Discounts all he has
divines a new arising
a doe-eyed glance
reaching, touching hands
hot breath on his eyelids
the feel of new and sweaty skin.

Anniversary

The First Wife

The two of us
dinner at our center pedestal oak table
grilled New York strip steak rare
red wine, dark chocolate dessert.

Look, you say
the apple orchard
graces our new home
the vintage carriage house.

October twilight dresses up the scene
displays a host of fallen apples
the kept promises of autumn
enticements to their wormy cousins.

We chatter on about the steak
stay cordial through the chocolate.
You don't suspect the thickened fumes
gathered in my gut.

My claim bursts out.
I quickly raise the steak knife
plunge it down into the table top
we'd painted apple green in better times.

The crash noise shatters dinner.
The fevered instant holds us
the knife stands upright in the table.
I look out, see you staring, mute.

I hoarsely croak
I'm sorry for the drama.
I should have told you.
I need to go away.
There's no one else.

Loved One

I found some time for you today
reached out

beyond the usual meanderings
to find you once again

dark and curly hair, peasant blouse
the laughing girl

who long ago conceded
you would go your separate way

that day I claimed
I needed to move on.

I sort through tattered recollections
we were not meant to be

losing touch with you these many years
because I did.

Now I try to put aside
the pinch of my regrets

make my way back
to our better times.

I'm told you've died.
You cannot hear me now.

Mother's Still

Last May we sat by the pool in plastic chairs
I praised the Ficus trees
cotton shapes drifted in the southern sky.

I reached out, held your hands
touched your bulging knuckles
caressed the purple roundness of your veins.

You moved your hand, your head lifted
a moment's frail connection
before you drifted off, silent as a cloud.

Your hours have no song or nectar anymore.
They pass like cats slipping furtive
outside of your screen door.

Your eyes stare fixed like hazel stones
the world shrunk to food and sleep
perhaps one random day a word you recognize.

I tend your wheelchair
guard the treeless plain inside your head
politely keep at bay well-wishing neighbors.

My patter wont dissolve the doctor's words
so clinical and certain
She's reached beyond the golden years.
Nothing to be done.

II.
Religion and Politics

Being First

Rich Guy Rhymes

The Wall Street Journal gives me swagger
      tells me I'm the biggest, richest
pumps me up with bragging rights
      how great it is to be the firstest.

Why it's great to be the first
      be the head of every line?
I never see the backs of others
      seeing backs is not so fine.

The upper part is where you see
      some neck and shoulder hair
blotchy, blemished, reddened skin
      shiny pimples here and there.

The lower part is even worse
      down near the butt is very bad
the cleavage there, it should not show
      when it does it's really sad.

So now you understand my friend
      why us rich folks have that thirst
why we need to make a fuss
      it's so important being first.

The Hand of God

Deist Prayer

The Old Testaments proclaim
If you accept His path to virtue here
His Kingdom surely will be there for you.
Accept our God who truly is your God.
Go our way. There is no other.

New Age Pundits state
There is no god, just particles
Ahead a dirt nap in forever.
The Here and Now is all there is.
Freedom's born with your embrace.

I turn away from all those voices
warmed inside my private faith.
You Are There
Behind the heavens' rhythms.
You set this all in motion then left us here

within the forests, oceans, mountains, deserts
cities, villages and lonely farms
the feel of rain and roses, babies skin
the smells of bacon, day-old socks
the honking noise of cars.

Your hand designed this tiny, so unlikely place
amid vast galaxies
endless cold and empty space
this earth, a gift
despoiled though it is.

I take Your hand
You vault me over walls of doubts.
You are benign, indifferent
enough
for my surrender.

Dust Bowl Troubadour

My Pen Pal Woody Guthrie

Ed,

I'm glad you reached out. It's good to be remembered.
How did I keep going all those years? Sure had me some days.
That dust all in my hair, even in my teeth.
Those bumpy back roads make you sore.

I wandered into lots of towns. Lost folks didn't see
the Dust Bowl coming. There was no prophesy.
The drought, that dust, came and didn't leave; farms dried up.
And then that evil twin the Great Depression.

So many out of hope, most days without a prayer
until their Sunday mornings they'd lean into their wistful God
after drinking through the night before, singing out with me
who surely is no God.

I'd set down in front of them, offer them some anthems.
Ain't Got no Home. This Land is Your Land.
Invite them all to sing along, maybe charge them up
for one more round of keeping on.

Maybe I was just a loco weed, worn off in the morning
but I do believe for some of those lost folks
I did get them up and going one more time.
That stoked me up
I'd brush that dust off one more time.

Thanks for asking Ed,

Woody

Grandmother of God

Dear Joseph,

I hope you know you are a blessing.
Forgive me for repeating
Lots of girls would marry a carpenter
Mary is a nice girl
But I did say look around, not just here in Nazareth.

I asked you more than once
What do we really know about her family?
What kind of dowry could they offer?
Is that a name for a Jewish girl?
You wouldn't listen.

You told me she's with child.
I thought you weren't trying.
Who knows how it happened.
And now, this trip down to Bethlehem,
Mary rides on your old donkey?

This time of year in Bethlehem is busy.
You should have known
There might not be an open room.
You're surprised you wound up in a stable?
Then the baby comes.

Angels visit, very nice.
You're happy with those shepherds?
Not a shekel to their name.
And those Three Wise Men
What kind of gifts are frankincense and myrrh?

Now you have a Holy Infant
You don't invite your mother?
I am to be God's Bubbe*
It really is a shonde.**
At least I have a grandson.

When are you coming back to Nazareth?

Your Mother

*Bubbe: Yiddish for "grandmother"
**Shonde: Yiddish for "shame"

Having It Out with My Guru about Old Age

And my life expectancy spreadsheets

You've offered me your wisdom,
Do not be afraid.
When that day arrives
you'll drop your body
your spirit will fly off
for a timeless time into The Void.

The Void?
An All-Inclusive-Destination for eternity?
No rooms with an ocean view
no in-pool cocktail bar
walking on the beach at sunset
a spa with music and masseurs?

Yes, The Void.
Take another, deeper look.
Eternity, no envy, anxiety or prejudice.
Believe beyond the message of your senses.
Watch your breath arise and fall.
Surrender all your clinging.
Do not suffer your attachments.

To loved ones who can scratch my back
Hold my hand, offer me a kiss
To the perfumes of croissants, apple pies and bacon
Tulip color riots, floating clouds of autumn leaves
The soft opening of summer mornings
The tender reach of baby pictures
The rhapsodies of Gershwin, Miles Davis?

These indeed are wonders
They all arise and pass away
Will not erase the moment of your body's end.
Do as I have counseled
Meditate upon the here and now
Cultivate the emptiness, the inner peace.
Do more walks and yoga

I do some walks and yoga
sometimes occupy the here and now
but emptiness is still elusive.
Just in case, I spend some of my remaining time
reviewing my investments.
Daily visits to my spreadsheets reassure me
when I'm 90, even 95
I'll still have enough if I arrive.

I Come from a Long Line Of

Slavic Jews, they are my people.
I proclaimed this to my first wife

lovely green-eyed Protestant
from another country, Illinois

that night when we smoked dope
way back in the day.

As always, she was quiet
seemed engaged

when I said *Slavic Jew*
explained in some detail

the Pale of Settlement, pogroms.
She'd heard about the Holocaust.

She was also quiet
3 years later on

did not insist or argue
with my brief announcement

when this Slavic Jew declared
I'm sorry
But I have to leave.

That Morning in the Queen of Peace Church

The Church, mystery on Main Street
one block from our Jewish home
Kew Garden Hills
my neighborhood in Queens.
When I was 10 years old

that sunny August morning
Johnny asks me
would I like to see inside the Queen of Peace
when he goes to "Take Confession."
Yes.

We yak up to the church
the heavy wooden door
the iron handle opens to a foyer full of candles
unexpected lights and scents
rise up to my face.

Johnny tugs me through another door
the center of the Church, the nave, he says
empty rows of dark wood benches
Catholic people sit and pray here
What they call *Sunday Mass.*

I say those words beneath my breath.
My eyes lift slowly
scan the rows of benches
up to stained-glass colored windows
further up into a sky-high vaulted ceiling.

Johnny leaves me gawking
walks away into a dark wood booth
disappears to "Take Confession"
with the Priest who he calls Father Jim
to confess about I don't know what.

Minutes later Johnny's out
comes back to where I sit.
I search his face, find no shining.
He nods for us to leave
we yak about a summer stickball game
jog our way back home.

Narcissus' Deal with the Foxes and the Weasels

The foxes in old Sunset County were in quite a tizzy
The farmers locked their chickens up in high tech chicken pens.
The foxes railed

It isn't fair.
The farmers have it in for us
They plot against us just because we're foxes.

Up steps that old fox Narcissus
Shouts *I alone can save you*
Promises he has a plan.

We need some allies; strength in numbers.
We'll team up with the weasels, even though they're weasels
They also love to eat the chickens.

Narcissus says to all the foxes and the weasels
I'll convince the farmers, their chickens will be bigger, plumper
When they make them free range chickens.

Hallelujah cry the Foxes and the Weasels too,
They'll all believe in free range chickens.
You will Make Us Fat Again.

Narcissus thinks *how great am I.*
The foxes and the weasels love me
I promised bigger, plumper free range chickens.

Now I'll dress up like a farmer (as only our Narcissus could).
Narcissus gets the farmers dreaming of the money, money
From their bigger, plumper free range chickens.

Narcissus woos them, wins the farmers over.
They set their chickens free.
The foxes and the weasels whoop it up

Pounce upon the free range chickens
Eat them with abandon
Until the chickens are no more
And the farmers look in vain for that old fox Narcissus.

The Times Square Prophet

Yo, you got a problem, me talking here to you?
You too good to listen, mister suit?
I heard you moan *fuck off.*
You could learn a thing or two
Even from us street folk.

We don't just mumble to ourselves.
I got a cell phone too you know
It called me, told me
I should share a secret
If you could spare a New York minute.

Listen, yeah to me.
I can give you something precious
The secret to a better life.
I could pass it on to you
If you would take a New York minute.

What I want? No money. Really.
I tell you what the secret is
And if you think I'm right
You nod to me, a little bow and then you say
You may be poor and smell like shit but you have got a point.

You game for just a minute?
Ok, Ok, here it is . . .
The secret is Be Nice, real nice to everyone.
There really is a God.
She's watching you and keeping score.

You know when you are losing?
If you don't know that God's a lady
She says *Count your friends*
Them people ask for nothing
Just your company.

So, what about it?
Be a mensch and I'll be on my way.
I'm waiting. Over here. Look at me.
A little bow and then you say
You may be poor and smell like shit . . .

Work Autumn Epiphany

I am a seasoned pro
strong enough to work full tilt
even in my sunset years.

My time is not yet up.
I'm better than the arrivistes
panting, impatient for their turn.

Project due dates
status updates every month
declare how good I am

until today
I hear about a colleague's failing heart
note another's bloodshot eyes.

I suddenly suspect
I've not outrun all of my suspicions.
There's quicksilver in my aspirations.

I am a water bug
swept down streams of memos and reports
tides of meetings, phone calls, texts and emails

my precious milestones collected
soon will be forgotten
like trivia and dead strangers.

I see the goodbye dinner
some toasts, kudos and good wishes
probably a plaque.

No public monuments
No caissons drawn by honor guards
No well-attended crucifixions.

III.
Meditations

Autumn Moment

Hints of an October stream
inside the hillside brush

draw me through a thicket
toward the supple flow

the dance of sunlight
flickers on its flowing skin.

I kneel along the bank
dip a hand into the cool

let it glide between my fingers
allow a slow-down moment.

Then I stand to snap a shot
and quick as that move on.

The stones within the stream
do not call me back

don't reveal how in their eons
the water wins them over

a rounded stone
lying in the stream bed

will surrender to the flow
journey over other stones

to quiet pools or muddy banks
with roots and vines exposed

or on into
an endless sea somewhere.

Deep Night Elegy

I wobble to the bathroom
my familiar path.
Before another round of sleep
I notice nearby hints of life.

Pale green glows in the alarm clock
Smoke detector twinkles on the ceiling
Stripes of moonlight tiptoe through the shutters
hover on our bedroom wall.

Outside
the other night world
scattered sounds
morph into invitations.

A commuter train, its hoarse laments
announce its muscular assurance
to deliver sleepy strangers
to their parking lots.

A truck engine's distant grinding
gear shifts whining higher, higher
calls out its journey
on a nearly empty highway.

The wind's breathing
slips through naked winter trees
rises, urges me to listen once and then again
take in its slow fall into silence

brings me back
into our night.

I turn my body on its side
let my eyes close

hear your breathing
through the soft throat of your slumber

drop down again
into my sleep.

Giraffe Whisperer

At the zoo was this giraffe
inside her fenced-in countryside
her head way up in the sky.
I watched her
followed her until

she noticed me
stopped grazing on the treetops
swung her neck around
in slo-mo she walked over
was coming over to me.

She brought herself up closer
nudged her head between the bars
placed her face where I could touch it.
I stood very still.
Giraffes are sometimes jumpy.

Real slow I moved my own face
up and past her oval eyes
near her ears, beautiful and twitching.
The twitching stopped.
I touched her cheek so soft

cupped my hands around her ear
so I could whisper to her
my next breath floated to her
nothing magic
I'm so happy you came over.

I felt my heartbeats
didn't want to keep her
paused before I drew my head back
another moment with her eyes.
And she looked back into me

stayed right there
a second
a second more
then she slowly raised her head
way up to the sky.

Late Winter Blues

Another February night
begrudges dawn
a pale sun inches up
onto the bottom of the sky.
Fragile light
foretells a shortened day.

Noontime crystal sunlight lures me
out among the frosted grass and naked trees
footsteps crunch the frozen earth.

Face skin aches, weary bones
petition for relief inside
before the dusk and night to come.

Sleep takes me to tomorrow
where kinder breezes waken
hibernated hopes for spring.

Then I remember
March and April cold snaps
slicing through still naked trees.

My aspirations wither.
I sit here in retreat
look out again
watch the the flimsy light.
The day dissolves into
another long, skin-drying night.

Mid-Day Musings

Lunch inside my office box

Inside my closing eyelids
the clamor of relentless emails, memos, meetings
fades away . . .

I'm at our redwood kitchen table
a little yellow cactus painted in each corner
safe harbor in my child's time

I walk among forever waves
an amber field of wheat
rolls inside an August breeze

Faces shine and smile
people I don't know
still I want to touch

Clocks float by
without hands
numbers more than twelve

A pair of stalking tigers
crouch forward
through a grassy hillside meadow

Close ups of their eyes
glow iridescent yellow
around black-eyed Susan centers.

Unannounced, their eyes dissolve
my body lurches
through a purple velvet tunnel.

Pouring out the end
into my office box
no tigers, tables, clocks or breezes.

I pinch my arm until it hurts.

Ode to Stargazer Lilies

I loved you that first day
your petals puckered like a lover's lips
a white and crimson satin robe
sash about to open

your brash display
fragrant perfumes
followed, prodded
I should bring you water every morning.

I was faithful
even when your outspread edges
grew those brownish traces

served you
through your wilting
in your final dying

pressed beyond my longing
winced before you

drew you from your crystal vase
laid you down on top of coffee grinds

to be carried off at dawn.

Retreat with *The New Yorker*

Weary from my self-inflicted uproar
yet another online meltdown

I sit among my house plants
no ties to anything

just the page I hold
coursing through cartoons, book reviews

a poem that guides me
How You Should Apologize.

Two unnoticed hours pass.
My legs ache as they unfurl.

I walk slowly to the front door
we just had painted red

step out into our neighborhood
breathe in tune with mid-March breezes

listen to them pass
through naked, patient trees.

Miracle of the Cantaloupes

In a Times Square restaurant I meet
and spend some time with old Farmer Leo
who takes a shine to this New Yorker
invites me to his melon patch
somewhere in Ohio.

At first sight I am dazzled.
Fields of dirt neatly combed in rows
lined with long green vines
sprout melons
all the way to the horizon.

A host of cantaloupes all risen
from his plain old dirt
because one day months ago
Leo pushed some seeds
down into agnostic soil.

Days and weeks went by
until a moment came when
out of sight the dirt
made love into the seeds
begat fruit babies in the dark.

Slow, but sure as days
came after one another
just when it was right
the dirt made room up top
a shoot, an inch of green

nudged up enough to soak in rain
and sun and shade and night
the shoots grew into vines
crawled inside the rows
branches budding yellow blossoms

and the blossoms swelled
turned somehow into melons
melons lay there in the rows
grew bigger, rounder
fill with sweet, pink-orange melon meat
all from Leo's dirt.

The Wisdom of Tuning into Bill Evans

who, when I call him
lifts me from my spikey trances
crackling rackets in my skull

snapping at this scaredy cat
turned this way, then that
by sudden barks from dogs I cannot find.

He offers me soft joys.
Sound temptations
arch their invitation fingers

subdue the din inside my skin
carry me into his tune
Waltz For Debby . . .

Where I float along her notes
follow rhythms
as they wrap around my room . . .

Bill at the piano, his bass guy and a drummer
playful, easy
I strum inside their harmonies

three masters
I invited
take me to a better place for now.

IV.
Aging

Big Boys Come Home

You're almost here, young, fatless, grown forever.
You used to crowd the doorway whenever I got home.
Now I wait inside the door for you.

Time is a wicked shadow.

I meditate to help me use up
less of my remaining life
inside regrets and fears.

Surrender is a tricky skill.

How are things going, Dad?
I say *I feel almost like I did 20 years ago.*
The problem is . . . I still can count.

You laugh at my familiar punchline.

I used to read to you in bed
taught you to ride bicycles
tended to your wounds.

I loved you more than I had ever guessed.

Now I hold the railing on the stairs
miss more things that people say
look forward to my favorite chair to sit in.

How much do you notice?

Empty Nest Arrangements

Glasses, pots and pans
tucked with care
inside maple kitchen cupboards.

Rose tinted granite counters
embrace stainless steel appliances
gleaming on the sunrise colored quarry tile floor.

The automated coffee urn waits patiently
beneath displays of plates and bowls hand-painted
tokens from our recent trip to Mexico.

Fresh cut lilies, roses, dahlias
brighten up the living room and dining room
favorite havens in our Cotswold Cottage home.

The coffee table picture book *Vermeer*
rests upon the rosewood butler's tray
balances the placement of an alabaster bowl.

Upstairs the beds are made, clothes tucked away
in proper racks and drawers inside the walk-in closet
nearby a master bath with heated floors and matching sinks.

These arrangements testify to wins
despite our sacrifices for the kids
helping them to grow and enter other lives.

Still, in unexpected moments
questions uninvited
slither in among our precious things.

I Think about the Lobster

He skitters on the bottom of a frigid ocean
spiny, cranky looking, fully grown
lifts heavy claws, flicks spindle legs
across the rocks and seabed, grey and gooey
the brown-black water
cold as an ex-lover's goodbye.

Everything is fine as it gets for lobsters
who don't know they taste as good as a first kiss.

Lured to an enticing morsel
munching on the herring bait
he's snatched up into the wind and sky
dumped into a black space
choked with ice
and other lobsters.

Later, maybe days, a rude white light splits the darkness
then the clamor of the lobsters skidding mute, down a metal ramp

followed by a hand
that grabs our lobster
straps a rubber band around his claws
drops him in a glass walled tank
among some other lobsters
plastic mermaids and a little castle.

The good news; lobsters cannot forecast.
But I can.

Now I'm fully grown.
If there is a God, please let me have my own life's shape—
my ocean, rocks, my grey and gooey seabed, friends and lovers.
Please, no sudden nets
no ice cold storerooms
rubber bands or plastic mermaids.

When I'm not looking
take me then.

Meeting Up with Never

I squeeze out from the plane
plunge into the din
arrival streams, departure throngs, PA squawks
food joints, bars and newsstands.

My iPhone vibrates in my pocket.
I hold it close
Your voice breaks through the racket
Eddie, Mom is gone . . .

I move aside.
stand there
waiting for my breathing
gulp an inhale.

I knew it would arrive
kept this moment in my attic.
Grief's insistence starts
I bump into my Never

when I should visit her
wheel her to the condo poolside
hold the bulging knuckles of her hand
chatter on about how warm it is.

Old Timer

He's made it to being old.
Less clocks
insistent calls to hurry up
be somewhere else.

This new morning
unfolds without a jump start
eyelids gently lift
he listens to his chest fill out

strums along inside his head
meanders in his musings
allows the urge to raise up
surrender to this portion of his shrinking life.

He creaks
laughs it off
parks it in his nurtured sense of irony
and the padding of memories.

Across his neatly ordered bedroom
on its proper stand his smartish phone
a comfort and umbilicus
plugs him into any world he chooses.

Handel or The Beatles
the playlist for today
his life a Greek diner
lots of choices on the menu

some not fresh
but choose we must
he picks one for no reason
nothing left to prove

less to risk
time has come to plug into his ear buds
so new to have nobody notice
lonelier but quieter.

Our Dying

Surely there will be my going black
some day not far enough away.
I should rave, will maybe shit myself
when I see it nearing to enfold me
the final slipping into darkness
the surrender to that vampire.

That night
      father's end closed in
      he left his bed and fell
      surely offered up no grace-filled musings
      cursed the god he swore was never there.

Two days late
      I come to see him lying mute, skin parchment thin and gray
      face turned up to the ceiling
      his open eyes are still
      fluorescence glows without judgment above his hospice bed.

There is no consolation for our dying
in biblical "hereafter" promises
or movie heroes "passing" gracefully
I've had a good run; time to go
see you on the other side . . .
Counterfeit concession speeches.

That final day
      He holds my hand, do I hold his?
      I watch as I stare silent at the window
      then at him, again at him.
      He lies there, mouth and body slack

That moment
    The final morphine dribbles into him.
    His chest now still.
    The darkness in his open speechless mouth
    I stare at it, remember
    sob for both of us.

Resolutions

Defiance at the dawn of my 80s

I will not kid myself.
I do wobble those first morning minutes.
hold on going up and down the stairs.
My right hand shakes my soupspoon.

I will surrender
to those hair tufts sprouting from my nose and ears
trim them so they won't obstruct
the power of my positive thinking.

I will make healthy choices
7,000 steps, 4 times, almost every week
eat more fruit and fiber, take no sugar in my coffee.
swear off giant cruise ships, hectic bus tours full of other geezers.

I will count all of my small wins.
Blood pressure's lower from that (small dose) med.
I do sleep well most nights, still with her
I gave up hope for cryogenics.

I will celebrate my senses.
My nose is still alert for that offering of bacon.
And if I'm still awake at 9:00 PM
I still can reach into my sleeping shorts
to find some satisfaction.

Fort Lauderdale Dilemma

I step into their condo
Mom reaches for my hands and says

I'm glad you're here, wish you'd visit us more often.
I have a question, just for you.
Remember Marty from Chicago?
He lives right there above us.

She points up to the ceiling
does not wait for me to nod.

Marty said he loves me.
He wants to run away.
We'll have money and the two of us
Should I go away with him?

The first moment of my visit
Should she run off with Marty?

Cloudy hazel eyes are fixed on me.
A upholsterer, retired, from Chicago
said he loves her.
Should she run away with him?

Mom and Dad together 50 years
gone through a lot, including one another.

Two of me go back and forth
she leaves and Dad unravels
she stays, adventure squandered
be open minded, guard the door.

She wants some spice
even in her golden years.

My next breath holds, escapes
I'm glad you shared this with me.
No wonder Marty's smitten. Pause.
But what a shock to Dad.

I think, advice well put.
I'm quite a lot like Solomon.

She sighs into the dishes in her sink
looks at me an eon later
I know, I know.
I wish that he was more romantic.

What I Will Be

I am ten, a skinny Jewish boy.
Every school day momma kvells
even though she wants me zaftig
rise and shine, my special boychik.
Her adorations tell me
I will be The Next Messiah.

At sixteen years, my boners
make their case against me being a messiah.
I never find a loving place for them except my hand.
I write down all my puberty's obsessions.
My fevered jottings tell me
I will be a famous author.

Thirty comes, no Pulitzers.
My nose befriends the grindstone.
I learn to burn the midnight oil
deliver quickly what I'm asked.
My swift promotions tell me
I will be rich and envied.

Midlife tiptoes in with no great wealth or fame.
I turn to smell the roses, savor veggies
love the tree shapes in their naked winters
calm my breathing with the hum of meditations.
My luminescent insights tell me
I will be a master of the Here And Now.

Now I'm old I'm told.
Hindus say *your spirit rises when your body drops away.*
I'm not convinced what lies ahead is such good news.
I do have episodes of some contentment
a good night's sleep
a moment with the morning sky.

I hope there's joy in proving nothing.

An Ode to My Older Brother

On Labor Day 2020 Mel died. After 20 years, cancer in his bladder spread out in his body. He could not even sit up. Now he was lying on a special hospice bed parked in the middle of his suburban New Jersey living room. The nurse sat quietly alongside him. His second wife, Paulette, was in the kitchen, preparing food for the family. His two kids gone outside, were waiting.

I came in the house, was standing over Mel. His red hair still in place like he always wanted it to be. Now it was dry, slate gray, streaked with red. I watched a few of those long, slow breaths. I tried to see the freckles in his hollowed face, stared at his hair, into the dark space of his open mouth. It closed. I squeezed my face. I tried to stop. I cried out loud, for both of us.

I went outside to be with the kids; they were together, under the oak tree in the yard. Danny was leaning against the tree, staring at the ground. Elena greeted me. "Hi Uncle Ed. I'm glad you came. How are you doing?" How typical of her, asking after others. An angel, I thought. Danny looked up from the acorns lying under the tree. "Yeah. Hi Uncle Ed. What a day!"

I didn't need to say anything. I looked at them; we all knew. There was to be a hole in our lives, no more Mel. Now he'd be memories I could turn to, soften if I needed to. When Mel and I were little, in Dad's photos he looked like the Gerber Baby. Mel has left us, but his family is here and I now am the oldest living member of that family. I do not feel like a patriarch.

V.
Epilogue

How I Keep Me Going

Cherish the morning window
Watch hawks float above the treetops
Slowly sip my coffee without sugar

Re-read Baldwin, Camus and Ram Dass
Highlight in yellow ideas I should remember
Attend an on line TedTalk on the Fear of Dying

Savor M's painting of the dark red dahlia
Watch a TV movie she says might be good
Rub her feet even when she dozes

Curate playlists; include Handel, Standup Comics
Visit Wikipedia, explore Glaciers, Vermeer
Ruminate on questions others think are silly

What will life be like if I do live to 120?
How will the boys look in their 70s?
Will there still be the filibuster?

Play iPhone solitaire to help me toward sleep
Be okay with those bathroom wake up calls
Sleep or lie in quiet 8 hours, maybe more.

Choose to be an optimist
I'll live through disappointment
Cry when I'm happy, even if it's public.

Say thanks when people listen, not just wait for me to finish
Be warm with friends, the folks who see me and still care.
Remember, I am safe inside this moment.

Author's Bio

Ed Ryterband was born in 1941 and raised in Queens, New York. His parents immigrated from Russia and Poland. He attended City University in New York, graduating in 1961, then went on to Purdue University where he got a Ph.D. with a focus on the psychology of leadership. His first job was as a teacher and management consultant in Athens, Greece. After he returned to the States, he continued to work in the U.S., Europe, Asia and Mexico. In mid-life, he left his career to become a stand-up comic, which he continued to do until he was asked to be a regular at The Comic Strip in New York. That was an offer he could not afford to take since he was married and now had a first son. It was then he returned to consulting and started to write poetry. His wife Madelyne and he have been married for forty years. They now have two sons, Jason and Michael, both grown and on their own. For the past thirty two years, Ed has lived at the New Jersey shore.

His poetry has been published in *Paterson Literary Review, Two River Times and U.S. 1 Worksheets*. He has performed his stand-up and poetry readings at *The Comic Strip, Mostly Magic* and *The Piano Bar,* among other venues in New York and New Jersey. His prior books of poems, *Life on Cloud Eight* and *Beyond Cloud Eight,* were published by Kelsay Books in 2018 and 2020, respectively.

ryterbanded156@gmail.com
www.edryterband.com

www.ingramcontent.com/pod-product-compliance
Lightning Source LLC
Chambersburg PA
CBHW032009080426
42735CB00007B/552